LIKE LEAVES

About this book

This book is written by the historian David Boyle, the author among other books of *Blondel's Song, Toward the Setting Sun* and *Alan Turing: Understanding the Enigma.* It was commissioned by the Friends of Battlefield Church and sold in aid of the church, which was built on the site of the original battle.

Like leaves fall in Autumn

Hotspur, Henry IV and the Battle of Shrewsbury

David Boyle

FRIENDS OF BATTLEFIELD CHURCH

Published in 2016 by the Friends of Battlefield Church
https://www.visitchurches.org.uk/visit/church-listing/st-mary-magdalene-battlefield.html
© Friends of Battlefield Church.

The moral right of David Boyle to be identified as the author of this work has been asserted in accordance with the Copyright, Designs and Patents Acts of 1988.

All rights reserved. No part of this publication may be reproduced, stored in a retrieval system or transmitted in any form or by any means, electronic, mechanical or photocopying, recording, or otherwise for commercial purposes without the prior permission of the publisher. No responsibility can be accepted by the publisher for action taken as a result of information contained in this publication.

ISBN (print) 978-1540351937

Contents

Prologue: *The dragon, the wolf, the lion and the mole*   1

I   A tale of two cities   5

II   The rebellion   17

III The battle   37

IV Aftermath   51

V   What next?   61

Appendix: Act V of Shakespeare's *Henry IV Part 1*   71

Cover illustration by Fern Chalcraft.

Foreword

I am delighted to be able to thank you for buying this book in aid of our church, and I hope it will inspire you to make a visit too. The field of peas where the battle took place is long gone, but the surrounding countryside of Shrewsbury is a beautiful place and well worth a day or a week away.

The church itself, dedicated to St Mary Magdalene, on whose day the battle took place in 1403, is a living memorial to all those who died in the battle. You can find us three miles north east of Shrewsbury. Access is off the A49 Battlefield roundabout which is next to the A5124 Battlefield Link Road. You will be able to find brown 'Battlefield church' tourism sign on the roundabout opposite the livestock market to guide you in.

I hope you will find there, as so many others have before, an authentic whiff of English history.

David Hulton Harrop
Chair, Friends of Battlefield Church

Prologue
The dragon, the wolf, the lion and the mole

There was a moment at the height of the Battle of Shrewsbury when it looked as though everyone, every knight and archer, every nobleman and peasant, would die there on that field of peas outside the city. Of all the battles on English soil, only the hideous slaughter of Towton, seven decades years later, saw worse bloodshed.

But Towton was made all the worse by mud and rain, though Shrewsbury in 1403 was also marked by heavy rain and floods in the weeks before. The reason Shrewsbury was so bloody was simple. The previous century had seen the development of a powerful weapon of war by the English and the Welsh and – for the first time in history – this was the battle that first unleashed the full power of longbow against longbow.

Twelve years later, the English archers would

decimate the French aristocracy and leave them lying on a field called *Carrion,* after the slaughter of the Battle of Agincourt, just as they had dominated the battlefield two generations earlier at Crècy and Poitiers. Now, in July 1403, the trained English and Welsh longbowmen faced each other, and before either side had developed any techniques to counter them. As the arrows rained down, one chronicler described the way the arrows cut down the soldiers like "leaves in autumn".

King Henry IV, still at the heart of the battle and before the debilitating illness that would turn him against his son and cut short his reign, had surrounded himself with nobles dressed identically to protect himself. Sure enough, one of them – Sir Walter Blount – was killed as the Scottish nobles led an assault deep into the royal lines. The Prince of Wales, the future victor of Agincourt, was hit by an arrow in the jaw, presumably bouncing off the armour of another knight. And amidst all that death, agony and destruction, the rebel leader, Harry Percy – known to history as 'Hotspur', the son and ferocious heir of the Earl of Northumberland – was killed, and nobody saw him die.

The result of this historic battle – let's not give it all away now – was that the Lancastrian royal line was saved, and the church at Battlefield was built over the bodies of those who had been felled, collected up from where they had been scattered over an area stretching for three miles, to commemorate the victory and pray for the King and the souls of those thousands who had died. There was also, perhaps, an implication that the daily prayers were to ask God never to allow such slaughter again on English soil.

He would, of course, because the seeds of the Wars of the Roses had been sown by this battle and by Henry IV's seizure of the throne four years before. So the grandchildren of those who first saw action at Shrewsbury, perhaps also numbered among the 'happy few' who fought with Henry's son on St Crispin's Day 1415, lived to see the nation torn apart in civil war.

But all that was for the future. The older generation at Shrewsbury were those who may have remembered as far back as Crècy, but who would have survived the Black Death and then witnessed John Ball, Jack Straw and Wat Tyler lead the peasants to London in revolt. They would have remembered the political turmoil which had gripped the nation by the throat in the years that followed, during the reign of the unpredictable and querulous grandson of the victor of Crècy and Poitiers, Richard II.

The actual revolt, like the deposing of Richard four summers before, was unexpected and must have been disturbing news, even for those who were immediately unaffected. It was another example of the aristocrats of England, hammering away above them like the gods of war – but involving them in their disasters as they involved all those who flocked to the rival banners in that long, wet summer of 1403.

I
A tale of two cities

"It was the best of times, it was the worst of times, it was the age of wisdom, it was the age of foolishness, it was the epoch of belief, it was the epoch of incredulity, it was the season of Light, it was the season of Darkness, it was the spring of hope, it was the winter of despair."
Charles Dickens, *A Tale of Two Cities*

It was the best of times; it was the worst of times. It was a time of peace and plenty and economic expansion; it was a time of war. And at the heart of the events which led to battle outside the city walls of Shrewsbury – as we have seen, one of the bloodiest battles in English history – was a bitter rivalry between the two medieval cities most closely involved, Shrewsbury and Chester, just up the border with Wales and on the River Dee.

Shrewsbury was a boom town. It had not reached the pinnacle of its wealth, but it was now heading in that direction, expanding rapidly because of the new industry of cloth.

The previous century had seen a major shift in medieval England's extraordinary economy, from wool production and its export to the use of wool in the new cottage industry turning it into clothing, or the dyed or manufactured fabric that would make it.

It had been Edward III, two generations before, whose advisors had recognised the potential of what economists call 'value added'. Why should the English simply export the wool, while the weavers of other nations allowed them to reap the growing financial rewards of turning the wool into dyed cloth or sumptuous clothes? The European economy would still take another three centuries to recover to the level of activity it had reached before the Black Death, but it was already clear that the rewards would belong to the most sophisticated, those who could transform their own raw materials – clothing and not just the usual English exports of wool and stockfish.

Wool had made England wealthy, but the Flemish weavers were proving you could still get rich on English wool outside England. Edward III had therefore managed to entice a number of Flemish weavers over from the Low Countries. One of the main causes of the Hundred Years War had been these struggles over the cloth trade.

But, here is why this was important for Shrewsbury: because Wales, having been such a lucrative source of the wool trade, was now key to Welsh cloth production, and Shrewsbury had positioned itself as the very epicentre of the Welsh cloth trade. It was on the River Severn, which was useful not just as a conduit for cloth and wool, but also for dying the cloth when it arrived. Shrewsbury's powerful Drapers' Company was rising to take on the huge power it was soon to exercise over the city in the centuries that followed, and it was the Shrewsbury drapers who came to dominate the market for Welsh cloth.

It was through them that the light Welsh cloth, known as cottons, friezes and flannels, came to the European market. The drapers of Shrewsbury would meet with weapons at the Old Three Pigeons Inn at Nesscliffe, and then would make the dangerous journey to Oswestry, deep into Welsh border country, to buy up the cloth to be finished and dyed. Then, every week, there was another packhorse train down the old Roman Road known as Watling Street to London's cloth market at Blackwell Hall. From there it would be bought by merchants and sent on to Rouen and the markets of the Spanish peninsular, and from there all over the known world. For the next three and a half centuries, until the turnpike roads of the 1790s, the Shrewsbury drapers remained the main route whereby Welsh cloth reached into the world.

By contrast, Chester was a city in serious economic decline. Their harbour was silting up, and that provided their only direct way to compete with Shrewsbury for the burgeoning Welsh cloth trade, via ship direct from Carmarthen. Otherwise, the roads from North Wales all bypassed Chester – and almost the only reliable roads had been built by the Romans and barely repaired since they had left Britain a thousand years before. Now the spread of the Welsh revolt, by a London-trained lawyer called Owen Glendower, had been eating into Chester's income in more ways than one. In fact, in the summer of 1403, Glendower was marching westwards into Carmarthen and Pembrokeshire, where Chester's corner of the cloth trade was sourced.

To make matters worse, because of Glendower's unexpected success, bylaws had been passed in Chester the previous year which restricted the movement of Welsh people. For a city that depended on trade between Wales and England, this represented a crisis for the city's struggling economy. And all the time, their southern rivals in Shrewsbury were getting richer and richer.

In the last years of the fourteenth century, Shrewsbury found itself drifting slowly into the camp that was most sceptical about the rule of Richard II. They had links with the hereditary lords of the Marches, the lawless areas between England and Wales, because this was the Mortimer family and young Edmund Mortimer was next in line to the throne, if the childless, unmarried Richard II was to die.

In fact, Edmund had a more powerful and obvious claim to the throne than Henry Bolingbroke, who was in those years in exile in France, worrying about what he could do to defend his landed inheritance if his ageing father

John of Gaunt, the Duke of Lancaster, was to die. But then, like all those towns which depended on trade with the continent, Shrewsbury wanted peace – they wanted the status quo.

Chester had less to lose and was anyway being taken to the bosom of Richard II, as his favourite city. The problem with Richard was that he trusted few people, but for some reason his heart went out to Chester. After visiting the city with the flower of English nobility in 1394, he selected two thousand Cheshire archers as his personal bodyguard. When parliament was held in Shrewsbury in 1398, Richard decided, "for the love he bare to the gentlemen and commoners of the shire of Chester" – not Shrewsbury, where he happened to be – he would now refer to it as a 'principality'. Richard II was in fact the first and only Prince of Cheshire.

As the heat of the last year of the disastrous fourteenth century began to rise, there was nervousness in England that the King was not securely on the throne – and his policy of peace with France might not also be entirely secure either. Those closest to Richard feared sometimes for his sanity. It wasn't that he was stupid – far from it – but he tended to fly into rages at mild slights or insults. And during one of these rages, he made the fatal error of doing precisely what his cousin, Henry Bolingbroke, feared the most. John of Gaunt died, and the exiled Bolingbroke inherited his title as Duke of Lancaster. But the King took the opportunity to seize the extensive lands of the Duchy, depriving Bolingbroke of his income and his base.

In England, there was a fervent excitement that something was about to happen. One poet called on Henry of Lancaster, the new Duke, in millennial terms, as "our light, our glory, our friend", urging him to return with Christ to save his people.

Henry was not an easy or an entirely secure man himself. He had endured a difficult childhood. His mother had died of plague when he was only a year old and he had been lucky to survive the Peasants Revolt at all, when John of Gaunt's Savoy Palace had been raided by the revolutionaries who had burst into London. He had been brought up by a succession of guardians in different places. But he was also clever, astute and a champion jouster who had seen military service with John of Gaunt, and with the Teutonic

Knights. He was also extremely wealthy, not just through his father's estates but via his wife Mary de Bohun, heir of the earldom of Hereford.

It has never been clear, when Henry sailed to England in the summer of 1399, whether he originally had any intention of going so far as actually to seize the throne. It may be that he was simply arriving to claim his inheritance. It may have been a happy accident that Richard and his closest henchmen were away in Ireland at the time. He had sailed with the agreement of Louis of Orleans, the effective ruler of France during this period of the long and disastrous reign of the mad King Charles VI. But Louis seems not to have considered the possibility that Henry might actually become King, and was furious when he discovered that was what happened. Either way, two weeks after their alliance, Henry was back in England.

He landed in Cromer in Norfolk and made his base at an abandoned settlement at the mouth of the Humber called Ravenspur. He very tentatively marched on his own castles, one by one across Yorkshire, and only when he was sure he had support did he dare to march south.

Richard also heard the news and hurried to return to the mainland, landing at Milford Haven on 24 July, and marching north to get to this favourite city. But Henry got to Chester first, promising to spare the county – aware of its powerful links with Richard and careful to keep the locals pacified. In the event, Henry's army ravaged the lands and villages of Cheshire anyway. He also had Richard's leading supporter Perkyn Leigh executed, and his head was stuck on a spike above the gate into the city. Chester would never forgive, nor forget.

It was fast becoming clear that the way to the throne was now open to Henry. His chosen instrument was to be the Percy family, cousins through their descent from Henry III, and the hereditary Earls of Northumberland, from where they policed the lawless border between England and Scotland. They were powerful magnates, father and son, Earl Henry Percy of Northumberland and his son and heir, Harry. The complexities of explaining the background to the battle of Shrewsbury are not helped by the fact that most of the key players are called Henry. This Henry Junior was known to history as much by his nickname as it was by the diminutive Harry. He was known to the world as Hotspur, and William Shakespeare would use that irony of the name to compare Hotspur, brave – not to say reckless – in battle, with the dissipated life of the other Harry, the future Prince of Wales who would become Henry V.

With Henry Bolingbroke was this third Henry, the Prince of Wales. Known to history as Henry of Monmouth – he had been born in the gatehouse of Monmouth Castle back in 1387, when his destiny in life had not been clear at all. Known to Shakespeare as 'Prince Hal'. We know he had a difficult relationship with his father, though he was just twelve when his father was crowned King.

In Bolingbroke's favour was the nervousness of the English aristocracy. Which way would Richard's rages take him? Would they suddenly find themselves, through some fatal misunderstanding, despoiled of lands, or worse? Now it was Hotspur's father, the Earl of Northumberland, who chose to act to bring Richard's reign to an end, but it was with an act of duplicity which clearly lay heavily on his conscience for the rest of his life.

Richard never quite reached Chester, at least of his own volition. He was safe inside Conway Castle in North Wales, when Northumberland intervened to offer him a safe passage to negotiate with Bolingbroke if he came out. Relieved that the rebels only wanted to negotiate, Richard emerged – but Northumberland had organised an ambush outside the city. He took Richard to Flint to await the pretender to the throne.

Northumberland claimed later that he had been deceived and that he had no intention of deposing the King. It may have been at least half true. Hotspur's nephew was the rightful heir after all, and Edmund Mortimer was now seven years old. Whatever the truth of the matter, Richard was taken to Chester Castle, jeered by a mob all the way and locked in the keep where nobody was allowed to speak to him. It was effectively the end of his reign and Northumberland and his family came to bitterly regret their part in the whole affair.

Parliament was recalled on 20 September and were read Richard's abdication document. They agreed that Henry should reign instead as Henry IV. Around the nation, towns and cities, the corporations met to agree the same thing. From Chester, there emerged a sullen acquiescence. From Shrewsbury, there was outright enthusiasm. They hailed Henry's accession "most joyfully and with our most entire will and heart".

The seeds of a second rebellion, and for the bloody battle outside Shrewsbury, had been sown.

II
The rebellion

"O that it could be proved
That some night-tripping fairy had exchanged
In cradle-clothes our children where they lay,
And call'd mine Percy, his Plantagenet!
Then would I have his Harry, and he mine..."
King Henry in William Shakespeare's *King Henry IV Part I*

The immediate cause of the rebellion that led to the field outside Shrewsbury was another battle, this one between an English army, led and paid for by Hotspur, and the Scots at Homildon Hill on 14 September 1402. It was one of those occasions when the English archers were unleashed against the Scots, with devastating results. Among those captured on the Scottish side had included

Archibald, Earl of Douglas, who had been blinded in one eye by an arrow during the battle, and whose valuable lands in the south of Scotland made him a hugely valuable captive, potentially earning enough ransom to pay for most of the campaign.

Within just over a week, King Henry – who had been transformed from a wealthy young heir to a perennially penniless King – had sent a message north forbidding the Percys to dispose of their prisoners. It was a slap in the face. The Percys had spent more than £20,000 on the campaign, a huge sum for the time – worth the equivalent of billions in today's values. They wanted some return on their investment.

Henry had only been King for three years, and was now painfully short of money. He had funded the business of taking the throne like the rich heir that he was, making huge and expensive grants of land to buy the support of Richard's remaining loyal backers. He had given the strong impression that he was not going to tax in the heavy way that Richard had taxed. In fact, most people believed he was not planning to tax at all. He had backed away from Richard's policy of peace with France, which implied that another ruinously expensive war was looming.

The French had been horrified to find that he had used their agreement with Louis to seize the throne, though they must have realised it was a possibility. If they had, they had not really considered the possibility that he might succeed. The French Charles VI had been mad since 1392, believing he was made of glass and therefore extremely fragile, supposedly sent over the edge into insanity by an accident at a ball when the flammable makeup on the guests had caught fire. He had taken to howling like a dog, which did not encourage confidence.

The French court were also now incensed that Henry had sent back Richard's child bride Isobel, but had done so without her valuable dowry. Henry had constructed a range of legitimate reasons why he had failed to pay it back, but the truth was that he had spent it.

To add to Henry's problems and his expenses, the Welsh revolt under Owen Glendower had capitalised on the simmering resentment of the Welsh against royal taxes. Glendower was actually a lawyer who had studied in Westminster but had managed to gather around himself something of the aura of a magician, and declared himself Prince of Wales.

To deal with Glendower, the fighting seasons had seen the real Prince of Wales – now in his difficult teenage years – learning about military matters along with his mentor, Hotspur, and between them leading the assaults in Wales. Prince Harry was gathering the reputation around himself that he was a playboy. Worse, there were rumours around that he had mugged his own citizens on the way into London.

So when the year 1403 dawned, it was a time – not just of great economic expectations – but also of great nervousness. Nervousness because those who understood such things were uneasy that the man wearing the crown had seized it by force. Expectations because there was now hope – partly because people widely believed that Henry had promised not to tax them (this was part of the reason for his financial difficulties) and partly because he was a dynamic new personality of whom much was expected.

It was also a period of rising tension. On 7 February, Henry married Joan of Navarre, the widow of the Duke of Brittany, in Winchester Cathedral, and she was crowned Queen of England three weeks later. Northumberland and his son made the journey from the north to Westminster Abbey to see it and Henry rewarded their support by finally granting them all the captured Douglas lands in the south of Scotland. There seems to have been no question of asking the Scots about this.

The coronation was one of those medieval spectacles, as the aristocracy with their coats of arms, clad in the very best dyed Welsh cloth, gathered in the draughty abbey to watch Thomas Arundel, Archbishop of Canterbury, lay the crown on the head of England's new queen. Joan was an accomplished diplomat in her own right and was able to get on both with the King and his difficult eldest son, and to liaise between them. But all the spectacle could not quite hide the fact that the aristocracy was divided, and especially disaffected was the Percy family.

Henry was not just leaning on the Percy family to defend his realm against the marauding Scots, he was also contracting them to manage the defence of Wales against the uprising co-ordinated by Owen Glendower. Nominally, the Prince of Wales was now sixteen and he was in command of the royal forces in Wales, and based in Shrewsbury. In reality, in the summer months, it had been Hotspur in charge, working in tandem with Prince Harry, teaching him about the art of war and being the mentor the prince so badly needed. The two had worked closely with each other.

There was something unnervingly fratricidal in Hotspur's attempt to target the prince and his tiny garrison that fatal summer of 1403. It is impossible to imagine that there wasn't some perceived slight, some bitterness, between the two men which made it possible for Hotspur to march on his young friend. For that was what was about to happen.

There certainly was bitterness between Hotspur and the King. It was part of the mysterious grudge of the Percy family, which began with the argument about the Scottish hostages but included a furious dispute about expenses. The King's treasury was by then seriously depleted. Who was going to pay for the enormous costs of fighting a small war in Scotland, let alone the defence of

Wales against a successful and widespread Glendowner uprising? Perhaps Henry felt there was some tacit swap that had been agreed in London that the Percys would pay in return for benefiting from the most lucrative benefits.

Either way, the two men met around the period of the Queen's coronation in London and there was a furious interview between them about the costs of the Scottish campaign, during which Hotspur is supposed to have drawn his dagger at the King. And as he sheathed it again theatrically, he is supposed to have muttered prophetically: "Not here, but in the field." In practice, the field was by then less than six months away.

There were also tactical differences which again hinged on money. Hotspur wanted the King to conciliate in Wales so that he could concentrate resources on the real issue, which was to keep the Scots in check – the Scots were after all threatening the hereditary estates of the Percys. It must have been through trying to organise some tentative communication links with Glendower that the outlines of an agreement between the plotters came to be made. It was then also, perhaps, that Hotspur and his father began to imagine the power they might wield over national policy if the nephew of Hotspur's wife, Elizabeth Mortimer, by then eleven years old, was on the throne instead of Henry the usurper. As we saw, young Edmund Mortimer had a greater claim.

The agreement was signed by all three sides, Hotspur, Glendower and the Mortimers. England was to be divided into three: Hotspur and the Percys would get the north, plus Northamptonshire, Norfolk, Warwickshire and Leicestershire. Glendower would get Wales and the West and the Mortimers would get the rest below the River Trent.

There was talk of Merlin's prophecy that the dragon and the wolf would help the lion rise against the mole. This was probably after the event, when it was said that these animals stood for Hotspur, Douglas, Glendower and Henry IV, though why the King was symbolised by a mole was never entirely clear. Nor does history explain why Hotspur's father, Northumberland, should have so quickly regretted his decision to back Bolingbroke over the rightful anointed king. Shakespeare suggests that it was the hot-headed Hotspur who drove the issue, but Northumberland had played such a key role in Henry IV's accession that it seems strange that he should cash in his kudos so quickly. Perhaps he had qualms about the trick he had played on the hapless Richard II.

Rather conveniently, as it turned out, the old Earl was ill and stayed on in Berwick. He claimed later to know nothing about Hotspur's plans but that is hard to believe. Perhaps he thought, as everyone else thought – apart from the initiated – that the army his son was raising in the early summer of 1403 was aimed again against the Scots.

It was a period of rising tensions, not just in the north but in the west. An urgent plea for help from Hereford had arrived in London to say that they were now threatened by the rebels. If Glendower had got as far as Hereford, on the border between Wales and England, then the situation was getting out of hand.

Armies in those days were becoming more professional. Ordinary soldiers would often sign on long-term, as the best guarantee that they would actually be paid. We can imagine that the kernel of Hotspur's army in the far north of England was made up of regulars who had campaigned with him many times before. He presumably kept it from them that they would be marching south this time – but then they had marched south many times before. Hotspur knew that he must not yet show his hand, but he knew about the rivalry between Chester and Shrewsbury and, this time, he planned to turn it to his own advantage.

In early July, he set off from Berwick together with Douglas, who had been promised his lands back if he would help the Percy family overthrow the monarch for a second time in four years, and together also with 160 mounted knights. He progressed carefully through Yorkshire and Lancashire, aware that the news must not get out about the direction that he was actually travelling.

The moment of revelation came a week into July. He arrived in Chester on 9 July and issued precisely the proclamation designed to most excite the locals. He announced that Richard II was still alive and that anyone who wanted to right the wrong, and overthrow the usurper, should join him in Sandiway, just east of the city.

Those who came to Sandiway expecting to see Richard again – and his dead body of the king who had most loved Chester had been exhibited in London, after all – were disappointed. What they actually found was another army, this time led by Hotspur's uncle Thomas Percy, the cantankerous Earl of Worcester. All who arrived with their longbows were enrolled into Hotspur's force, which was preparing to march south.

The men and archers of Cheshire certainly rallied to the cause. It was no coincidence that Hotspur's new enlarged force was being called on to overwhelm their great rivals on the River Severn, at Shrewsbury. Because, as everyone knew, Shrewsbury was the Prince's headquarters and there was an opportunity to take him on and his small garrison before anyone really knew what was happening, and then to link up with Glendower's army.

As far as the royal authorities were concerned, Hotspur was making his way north to deal with the Scots, or at least south to discharge his royal duties. Only Chester knew otherwise. And, although the Prince may have had an inkling of what was on his way – the trauma of a murderous attack by his old mentor – the King was safely in London and ignorant of this bid that was about to bring his short reign to an end.

But the King was not in London. In fact, the previous week, Henry had changed his mind. The desperate request for help from Hereford had unnerved him. He knew that Hotspur was gathering an army and he had considered that, after Homildon Hill, there was no need for him to take the field that year. But he now feared the worst and was even then marching north through the Midlands in the gruelling rain, ostensibly to support Hotspur against the Scots.

When Hotspur was collecting his Cheshire archers in Sandiways, on 12 July, the King was in Nottingham and it was there that he heard about the revolt and Hotspur's proclamation in Chester. Something was going on. In Burton-on-Trent, he made his first moves – urgent messages to the City of London to organise loans to pay for a defence, and sending a spy immediately to Hotspur's camp. But Henry was a seasoned military campaigner himself and he knew the score. Everything now depended on speed and his ability to drive his men fast for 30 miles to make up the distance between them. If he could close the gap and get to Shrewsbury before Hotspur, then he could rescue his irritating eldest son.

A medieval army on a forced march was a tremendous sight, as the troops began to leave behind their wagon train and their retainers. The mounted knights with their banners and coats of arms, the professional soldiers and the archers, with their distinctive bows and quivers, began to accelerate, complaining and swearing in the damp July heat.

The historian David Green described the other people who would follow on behind, the army hangers-on, "pavillioners, grooms, cooks, stablemen, cordwainers, wheelwrights, fletchers, bowyers, saddlers, arrnourers, clerks, tailors, miners, stonecutters, smiths, waggoners, physicians, and surgeons". Edward III used to take thirty falconers with him in his entourage on campaign, and some of this army of support staff would have served with him. These now faded into the dust behind as the King's fighting troops took to the road towards Shrewsbury.

By then, Hotspur and the Percys were making their way south from Chester and entered Shropshire through Whitchurch, arriving outside Shrewsbury on July 19, demanding to be let in so that the army could be fed. But Shrewsbury's corporation stuck to their allegiances and barred the gates of the town. Hotspur and his combined army were forced to camp two miles outside the city at Bullfield Common.

Hotspur had been relying on intelligence about Henry's progress north and last heard of him in Burton-on-Trent, where he assumed he still was. This time, it was Hotspur's turn to be surprised. Henry had left Burton three days before and had headed for Lichfield to collect more troops, sending out his sheriffs from there to the surrounding counties, to collect more. Since then, as we have seen, he had been marching with all speed towards Shrewsbury, guessing correctly that Hotspur would be trying to take the garrison there, take his son captive and head on into Wales.

The day that Hotspur arrived outside Shrewsbury, the King and his rapidly growing army was at St Thomas' Abbey in Stafford. The next day, they marched as soon as the sun had risen and arrived at Shrewsbury in the morning. This time, the gates were opened and they marched straight into the city. Hotspur had spent the night with the Betton family in the village

Upper Berwick. He was staggered to get the news that the King's banners had been seen.

The pressure was now on the King to prevent Hotspur from joining with Glendower's army, which both of them assumed to be nearby. In fact, Glendower was nowhere near Shrewsbury. He was marching into Pembrokeshire at the time, in the far west, one of the reasons for his reputation as something of a knave.

The plan the next morning, Saturday 21 July, was to send the Prince with a small force to root Hotspur out of Upper Berwick, while the main army marched out of Shrewsbury by the city's Foregate, crossing the River Severn at Uffington to cut off Hotspur's retreat to Chester. Unable to go into Wales or escape to the east, Hotspur planned to withdraw tactically to the north, and his army – by now in some disorder – began to make its way through the villages of Harlescott and Albright Hussey and into the field of peas known to history as Hateley.

It was clear that he was going to have to fight, and there was a very slight incline here which had possibilities for defence. He placed his troops behind the peas and there the two armies rested across from each other. It was only midday.

If it actually came to fighting, it was clear that Hotspur had more of an advantage than was immediately obvious. The peas were planted in canes which obscured the view once you ran into them. In those circumstances, his archers would have an advantage if he had the sense to stay where he was. The real question that Hotspur was agonising over, and which Henry was also asking himself, was this: where were Glendower and the Welsh rebels? With Glendower on his side, Hotspur could certainly afford to fight, but where was he exactly? We have to imagine him sending scouts out to the west, desperate to find out. As we know, of course, Glendower was nowhere near, being apparently unaware that Hotspur had actually acted. In fact, that very day, Glendower was consulting a fortune teller in Carmarthen, and between him and Hotspur the valleys were flooded. Even if he had wanted to come, he could hardly have done so easily.

Shakespeare imagines an exchange between the two men as they planned their joint campaign, which brings out the caricature of both of them – Hotspur hotheaded and sceptical, Glendower pompous, vainglorious and fake.

"I can call spirits from the vasty deep," says Glendower, boastfully.

"Why, so can I, or so can any man," replies Hotspur, at the end of his tether. "But will they come when you do call for them?"

"Why, I can teach you, cousin, to command the devil…" says Glendower in the same vein.

Shakespeare was responding to Glendower's extraordinary reputation for magic, unusual for someone who had been trained in Westminster. He was widely supposed to have the power to make himself invisible. We might imagine Hotspur's bitter quips, as he faced the field of peas, that Glendower's invisibility now extended to his entire army.

War is said to be a contrast between long periods of boredom and moments of fierce, intense and frenetic activity. The boredom part was about to begin and Hotspur sent his two squires, Thomas Kneyton and Roger Salome, over with a letter to the King, signed by his father and his uncle, accusing him of breaking his oath, of starving Richard II to death, usurping the throne and levying taxes without the permission of parliament. It was a kind of public declaration of intent.

Henry did not want to fight if he could possibly avoid it. He knew that one of the most effective military commanders in the kingdom was now opposing him, together with a fearsome force of Cheshire archers. Nobody could predict the outcome. It was clearly time to see if he could avoid a battle, so he sent Thomas Prestbury, the Abbot of Shrewsbury and the Abbot of Haughmond to the rebel army with an offer of a pardon to Hotspur and his associates and offering to redress their grievances. Unfortunately for both sides, the abbot was directed – not to Hotspur – but to the uncertain temper of Hotspur's uncle Thomas, the crotchety and ill-tempered Earl of Worcester. Otherwise the outcome of the day might have been very different.

It took time for the discussion in both sides and it took time to send messages back and forth between the two lines, but by late in the afternoon, the King's side began to be suspicious. They knew that Hotspur was inclined to accept the offer of peace, but his uncle Thomas was dead set against it. It began to look as if they were deliberately stringing out the negotiations while they waited for Glendower.

At that stage, after negotiating for most of the day, that George Dunbar, Earl of March, advised the King that the rebels were just playing for time. He then pulled out his ace card: he said he believed that Hotspur wanted to be King himself. "As long as I remain alive, I swear that will never be," said the King. "In the name of God, take the banners forward."

Hotspur was also beginning to fear the worst. A few hours earlier, he became aware that he had forgotten his sword. He was told that he had left it at Upper Berwick. Hotspur had not heard the name of the village where he slept the night before, and he is said to have turned pale, aware that it was also the name of his home city. He had received a prediction some years before that he would die in Berwick, and assumed that had meant at home and in his own bed.

"My plough I see is reaching the end of the furrow, for it was told me by a seer, when I was in my own country, that I should verily die in Berwick," he said. "But woe to me, the double meaning of the name has beguiled me."

III
The battle

"How much more complex than this is the game of war, which has to be played out within specific time limits, and where there is no question of one man's will directing events through his control of soulless machinery, because everything develops from the interplay of infinitely varied and arbitrary twists and turns!"
Leo Tolstoy, *War and Peace*

There are no photographs of course, and no paintings of the battle conceived by Victorian artists to bring it alive, but we have to imagine the two sides ranged against each other as they waited for a decision – would they fight or agree? Would they live or die?

So we have to conjure the scene as the two armies faced each other, their pennants swaying in the July heat, their coats of arms on their breastplates within sight of each other, the occasional flash of sunlight on polished metal. There was the blue lion rampant of the Percy family, and the soldiers of his own household wearing Hotspur's personal symbol of the crescent moon. There was the quartered royal arms of the three lions and the French fleur-de-lys of King Henry (his grandfather, Edward III, had first quartered his arms with the French royal coat-of-arms to demonstrate his claim to the French throne). There was the bright yellow and red of the Stafford arms, and the white stars on a blue background and the red heart, which demonstrated the presence of Archibald, Earl of Douglas.

We have to imagine the breeze in the trees and in the faces of the archers as they peered at their targets across the trees, waiting for the order that would lead them to reach into their quivers of arrows and put one to the string, as they had practiced so many times. Or the sweat on the face under their armour, or boiled leather protection.

The question of how big the opposing armies were has obsessed historians ever since. One suggestion is that Hotspur's army, now the smaller of the two, numbered 14,000. Other contemporary chronicles suggest that the royal army was about 60,000 strong. This now seems to have been a huge over-estimate and recent histories have put the numbers much lower, as you might expect from two armies that had both been cobbled together rather hastily. There is some evidence from the very precise, though conflicting, figures given for the dead: these ranged from nearly two thousand to over three thousand. We also know that the death toll was high compared to other medieval battles.

Most armies of the time were half infantry and half archers, and using the most powerful military weapon in Europe at the time – the English and Welsh longbow – which suggests that somewhere between 5,000 and 15,000 archers now faced each other across the field of peas.

Longbows were not exactly new technology. They had been developed in Wales but first used by the English to devastating effect at the Battle of Falkirk in 1298, when Edward I beat William Wallace. It was amazing, in fact, what a six foot piece of ash or yew could do over a range of about

400 yards. The English archers in every village were now only too aware of their importance in the defence of the realm – and, since 1365, they had been forbidden to leave England without a licence. The export of either arrows or bows had also been forbidden.

The arrival of the longbow as the decisive weapon also implied a huge social shift was taking place. For the first time in history, battles were won – not by the massed aristocracy charging on their warhorses, as they had been won by Richard the Lionheart – but by the peasants with their bows and their home-made arrows. The victory at Homildon Hill had been won, according to one chronicler at the time, by "unremarkable poor men and serfs". Gunpowder was beginning to be used too and, again, it was in the hands of trained peasants. Victories were being engineered by the poorest of the poor, but trained into a fighting force.

This meant a change to the way that armies were recruited. As we have seen, both Hotspur and the King had recruited professional archers and infantrymen who formed the core of the small armies that faced each other across peas that day.

It was also a period of history when ordinary people were waking up to their power. The Peasant's Revolt had been only two decades before, though that had mainly been led by the emerging middle gentry, and ordinary people had been closely involved too. The traders in the cities, the professional bowmen, the labourers aware of the labour shortage after the Black Death a generation or more before – they were all waking up to their critical importance to making anything happen. They were beginning to understand their market power for the first time.

As a result, they were beginning to wear whatever clothes they liked, rejecting the hated *sumptuary* laws of chivalry which had regulated the colours each strata of the class system was allowed to wear. They were earning more. It was an uncomfortable moment, and somehow the ability of a nobleman to unseat a king, and to put him to death, must have increased that sense that the world was turning very slowly upside down.

What was happening to England, they asked themselves, if the plague had killed a third of the population, if the peasants and risen in revolt, if kings and usurpers faced each other across a field of canes – and all within living memory? What was happening to people's place in the world?

This was especially a consideration for a King who was chronically short of money, when a standing professional army, or contracted mercenaries, were an additional expense which he simply could not afford, but which he could not afford to forget either. Armies were increasingly expensive things in this new world.

The longbow was still pre-eminent, but there was also a new twist to military technology at the time. No armour could withstand a direct hit from an arrow, but increasingly the knights and even their professional men-at-arms were wearing plate armour to prevent the kind of wound that Prince Harry was about to suffer in the face, from a glancing blow. So a new weapon had been developed which could smash its way through plate armour and was wielded by an infantryman. The new weapon had been developed was the poleaxe, which could be swung at great speed to break through plate armour. It was a fearsome thing.

The poleaxe and the longbow together meant that the first mover was at a serious disadvantage, as they would be again in the First World War five centuries later. The key to victory, as it would be at Agincourt a decade later and as it was at Shrewsbury, was to use your archers to provoke the other side into launching at attack. But the Hotspur was quite experienced enough to know this. He knew what he had to do.

Two hours before the dusk, in the early evening, Henry began the battle by raising his sword. There were shouts from both sides as he did so. The trumpets blew and there were shouts of "St George!" from the King's side – St George was now firmly ensconced ahead of St Edward the Confessor as the English patron saint. Then there were answering shouts from the professional men-at-arms on Hotspur's side, who shouted the Percy war cry: "Esperance Percy!"

The shouts were followed by a hail of arrows from the archers on both sides. It was this, above everything else, which led to the slaughter. It was immediately clear, as well, that Hotspur's Cheshire archers had the upper hand, thanks to the slightly raised position that Hotspur had chosen for the battle. The King's men "fell like leaves in autumn," wrote the chronicler Thomas Walsingham about the deadly barrage from the men of Chester. "Every one struck a mortal man!"

The royal army was now drawn up on slightly lower ground, unable to see very well over the peas, with the King himself commanding the centre of the line, and his son Harry in charge of the left wing. The twenty-five year-old Edmund, Earl of Stafford, was commanding the right.

The hail of arrows was devastating. On the left side of the King's lines, Prince Harry received an arrow in the jaw, bouncing off the armour of a man next to him. Realising the gravity of the situation, and in great pain, he insisted on staying on the field of battle. He broke off the arrow shaft and stayed put. On the right wing, the situation was increasingly dire. An arrow killed Stafford outright and those around him fled. The chronicler talked about the first wave of arrows and the men around the King falling "like leaves that fall in the cold weather after frost".

That was just the first wave. Soon there was another and another. Hotspur must have looked down from his incline with satisfaction as he watched a portion of the King's right flank turn away and escape in confusion. He would have been less pleased to see a part of his own force marching, against orders, over to the King's side, and he must have cursed Richard Rankyn as a traitor, having clearly agreed secretly to switch sides once the battle was under way. The front ranks on the King's side, warned what would happen, opened to let in Rankyn's men.

Even without Rankyn and his contingent, it must have been clear to Hotspur that he still had the advantage. All he needed to do was to stay on his ridge and fire arrows down into the King's men below. So why didn't he?

This is the central mystery of the Battle of Shrewsbury. If Hotspur had stayed where he was, history would have been different. But that was hardly Hotspur's way. He may not have been the hot-headed, uncompromising northerner who Shakespeare portrays, but he was above all a man of action. He chafed at standing still and something seems to have happened to draw him and his men down into the melee. What this seems to have been was the movement by the Scots.

What happened was that the Scottish leaders who Hotspur had taken prisoner and the Battle of Homildon Hill were now allied to him and on the front line of Hotspur's army, having agreed to a deal whereby they could earn their freedom by fighting for him. It seems to have been the Scots who broke and forged down into the field of peas. Hotspur may have felt that he owed them his support – this was the age of chivalry, after all. He could not just leave them down there to be cut to pieces by the royal bodyguard.

But there is another possibility. It may have been that the prospect of finishing the battle in a pro-active way – taking events by the scruff of their neck – was just too tempting when Hotspur could see the royal colours flying over the peas. There was the King, only a few hundred yards away and in plain sight, in the midst of his troops. Hotspur knew that an experienced soldier like himself, with adequate support, could forge his way in, kill the King and end the battle.

Whatever the reason was, Hotspur left his ridge and slashed his way with the Scottish aristocrats, right into the heart of the King's army. He did not know, as we have seen, that this move had been anticipated – perhaps it was Hotspur's trademark heroism – and there were four pretend kings, dressed identically, ready for just such a threat.

One of these, Sir Walter Blount, was now killed outright by Douglas himself.

It was at this point that Prince Harry, still in intense pain from the wound to his face, made his decisive move, aware that this was the moment to act. He turned his wing of the royal army around 90 degrees and attacked Hotspur from the side.

Hotspur must have realised at this stage the peril he faced, having abandoned his safe spot on the ridge. He and Douglas were still surrounded by 30 knights, and they advanced now on the real King to finish the issue between them. It was clearly now a matter of minutes before he would miss his great opportunity.

Three of Henry's bodyguards were killed in the melee. The royal standard was flung onto the ground. Henry's horse was killed under him and, at this moment of confusion, his life was saved by the intervention of Dunbar. This gave him a moment's breathing space to send a message to his strategic reserve to come into the battle.

It was then that the rebel leader, still in the thick of the fighting, was hit by a spear blow or an arrow in the head. One story suggested that Hotspur was hit in the face with an arrow when he opened his visor to see more clearly. Whatever it was, nobody around him saw the fatal blow. The confusion was anyway now intense.

When some of the Northumberland knights saw Blount lying dead in the royal coat of arms, they shouted for Hotspur and proclaimed him as king: "Henry Percy King!" they bawled above the noise of battle. Battles are won and lost with shouts of this kind. It required decisive action. Henry himself heard them and shouted back "Henry Percy is dead!"

Whether he knew this or not, whether he was making a desperate last gamble to avoid panic on his own side, is not clear. The Northumberland knights waited for the inevitable answer from their own leader and there was none.

Was Hotspur dead after all? It wasn't clear. The knights searched desperately for him. Nobody had seen him go down. But it was too late, and the rebel army began to panic. Those who could do so began to slip away across the fields. Those at the heart of the battle began a more ordered withdrawal and it quickly became clear that, in a battle which had lasted just three hours, the King's side had won after all.

As the night began to fall, it was still not clear to many of those who had been taking part in the battle which side had been victorious.

IV
The aftermath

*"This, Douglas? no: I know this face full well:
A gallant knight he was, his name was Blunt;
Semblably furnish'd like the king himself."*
Hotspur disappoints Douglas, explaining he has not killed the King after all, in Shakespeare's *Henry IV part 1*

As the light faded from the field of peas, the victorious army began to turn their attention to collecting the bodies of the dead. Thanks to the chase that had taken place as dusk fell, an attempt to catch and kill the rebel soldiers as they tried to escape, the bodies lay over an area of about three miles.

As we have seen, the chroniclers were very precise – but varied – about the numbers of the dead who were buried. One report put the figure at 1,847. Another said it was 2,291, and another said authoritatively that it was, 3,460. Whichever was true, a mass grave was dug nearby measuring 100 feet long, 24 feet and 12 feet deep. It was a huge undertaking and it had to be done quickly before the bodies putrified in the July heat.

Even at that time, the angry Chester contingent was taking a small revenge on the King. As they escaped from the battlefield, they came across the enemy baggage train, and stole as many as 7,000 horses, which they took with them as they hurried north.

The heir to the throne had the remains of an arrow sticking out of his face. The physician-general John Bradmore took on the task of designing and making a special implement for extracting it from the Prince's jaw, which he did by boring a hole in the flesh and dragging it out from the bone. It must have been excruciatingly painful, and the wound was then disinfected and calmed with a mixture of honey and alcohol. Prince Henry had a distinctive scar on his face for the rest of his life.

The chroniclers suggest that about a third of

those who had taken part in the battle had been killed, which suggested either much more dead buried elsewhere or much smaller armies. Either way, there was now a long list of dead gentry and aristocracy on both sides – civil wars are painful events, after all.

On the King's side, Sir Hugh Stanley lay dead, so did Sir John Clifton, Sir Hugh Mortimer, Sir Richard Sandford – the list goes on: the royal side seems to have sustained far more casualties. The Earl of Stafford, who left behind a wife and three young children at home. On Hotspur's side, there was Sir John Massey, Sir William de Legh and Sir Gilbert Halsall and many others.

Hotspur's body was easily identified by the blue lion rampant on the surcoat, and it was clear that he had been killed by some kind of blow to the head. It was a poignant moment for both sides. There was no chance for Prince Harry to say his eulogy over the dying Hotspur, as Shakespeare has him do. But the King was taken to see the body and he wept. He had cared about Hotspur, admired him even, and had trusted him to mentor his own eldest son.

The King's mood at this stage, and his first

instincts were merciful. He wanted to save the life of Hotspur's uncle, the Earl of Worcester, but was advised that Worcester's was a clear case of treason. He had been a knight of the garter and should have been bound by the oaths he had taken.

So Worcester, together with Sir Richard Venables, Sir Richard Vernon and Sir Henry Boynton were beheaded at High Cross in Shrewsbury two days later, on 23 July. Worcester's head was sent to London where, by hideous tradition, it was stuck up above the southern gate to London Bridge. There it stayed until 18 December, when it was taken down to be buried with his body in Shrewsbury Abbey. The heads of Venables and Vernon were sent as a warning to Chester and stuck above the city gates there.

The King then collected his army and his long group of retainers and military and non-military hangers-on, strung out with the baggage train all the way back to Burton-on-Trent. Then he headed north to confront Hotspur's father, the ailing Earl of Northumberland. The old man sat in Berwick awaiting his fate, bitterly protesting his innocence.

He had no idea what his son had been planning. Really, he had been ill and had not the foggiest what was being planned by his headstrong eldest boy…

Thinking ahead and trying to avoid another risky confrontation, Henry asked the old man to come to meet him at York and to submit, without his retainers, and his life would be spared. Northumberland grasped at the opportunity with both hands.

As for Hotspur's body, he was buried at Whitworth nearby, by his nephew, Thomas Nevill, Baron Furnival, but that had been during the brief period of the King's mercy. When Henry had been convinced otherwise, Hotspur was exhumed again and put on display, salted and impaled on a spear between two millstones in the centre of Shrewsbury, on a spot later occupied by the post office in Pride Hill. When people had seen their fill, his body was beheaded and cut into four quarters and these were sent to the mayors of London, Bristol, Newcastle and Chester. His head was sent to York and put on top of the north gate staring northwards with unseeing eyes, towards his own lands.

Then, by early November, the King had relented. He agreed to put the bits back together again and to send the body back to Hotspur's widow Katherine, to be buried in York Minster.

Those who had supported the rebellion had their lands confiscated. But on 3 November, the day the King had made his offer to Hotspur's widow, he agreed to a royal pardon for the men of Cheshire, in return for a payment of 300 marks, and for the men of Chester again on the same basis. Three weeks later, he agreed to a general pardon for anyone as long as they asked for one before epiphany the following year.

While all this was going on, the work was still taking place to deal with the bodies of the dead. The aristocracy and gentry who had died in the battle were buried at Augustine Friars in Shrewsbury. For the rest, in the mass grave, the solution seemed to be to raise a church near them. And so it was that a chapel at Battlefield was built to commemorate the battle and Henry's lucky victory, and it has been assumed by historians that it was built over the huge mass grave dug to accommodate the bodies.

The chapel was dedicated to St Mary

Magdalene, aware that the battle had been fought on her saint's day, 21 July. Roger Ive, the local rector of Albright Hussey, also a staunch Lancastrian and therefore a supporter of Henry IV, took charge of the organisation and said services there every day for the salvation of the King's soul and for those who had been killed and buried there.

Ive also agreed to turn the chapel into a church, still there today, as well as running an establishment with as many as eight permanent chaplains, together with a college next door, and to hold an annual fair on the same site – presumably to pay for the chaplains and upkeep – every year on 21 July. The grants were confirmed by the pope in 1411, in the middle of a three-way split in the Papacy; agreement eventually came from the soldier anti-pope, John XXIII. Ive became master of the chantry.

By then, the church had been built in the perpendicular style, the English form of late gothic. The tower was begun in 1444, the year that Ive died, and finished in 1503. There was originally a rectangular moat around the church and outbuildings, the remains of which have never been found.

In the great period of privatisation, under Henry VIII, after the dissolution of the monasteries, when religious houses and endowments were seized by the crown for onward sale, the chantry and the small chapel on the side of the fair was sold off. It was bought by the local landowner, Richard Hussey. Battlefield church became the parish church for Albright Hussey and the field next door was set aside for the annual fair, which carried on into the 1840s.

It was never clear what happened to the attached almshouses for the parish. The bells were also carried off and sold to St Mary's, Shrewsbury. By then, the church had fallen into a pretty terrible state: the roof had fallen in and the weather was doing its share of damage. In 1749, the first attempt was made at restoration. The stained glass was removed for its own protection while a new roof was built and was looked after by a local farmer, who broke it.

A century later, the roof had fallen in again and only the chancel was being used for services. It was only in the late 1850s, when antiquarian restoration was suddenly all the rage, when the money was raised for a proper restoration and a new roof – and a new bell. The work was finished in 1861 and the church was rededicated by Samuel Wilberforce, the controversial bishop of Oxford who had recently been bested in a debate about evolution with the supporters of Charles Darwin ("Is it on your grandfather's or grandmother's side that you claim descent from the apes?" he is supposed to have said).

When a drain was put in on the north side of the chancel in the nineteenth century, the workmen involved found themselves cutting through layers of human bones. Other bones were found under the floor when the church was being restored around 1860. It seemed to confirm the story that the great grave lay beneath or near the church.

V
What next?

"For worms, brave Percy: fare thee well, great heart!
Ill-weaved ambition, how much art thou shrunk!
When that this body did contain a spirit,
A kingdom for it was too small a bound;
But now two paces of the vilest earth
Is room enough…"
Prince Harry to Hotspur's body in Shakespeare's *Henry IV part 1*

The old Earl of Northumberland, Hotspur's father, came tentatively south on the King's orders, after wintering in the north. He came before Parliament, who gave him the benefit of the doubt. He had risked a brief interview with the king, who had promised to spare his life but did not extend the same benefit of the doubt. Henry owed his throne to Northumberland, but that was not a comfortable feeling to have about someone who had clearly been plotting against you.

So Henry had Northumberland locked up in London, and sent his officials north with orders for the surrender of the Percy castles across the north and border regions. One group of Hotspur's knights, back from the Shrewsbury battle, refused to surrender them for more than a year.

In London, there was genuine uncertainty about Northumberland's guilt and some sympathy with him at the royal court. It was only too obvious, just looking at the King and his eldest son, that royal or aristocratic authority did not always extend to their children. There was also a nervous acceptance in London that Henry needed the authority of the Percy family to protect the north and to hold the Scottish border.

So, after some months of incarceration, Northumberland was fined and pardoned. He was also given back his lands and titles, at least all those lands he had held up to the end of Richard's reign in 1399. He was also not allowed to keep the wardenship of the Marches. They would no longer rely on the Percys to hold the line against

Glendower. Later, in 1404, Northumberland was ordered to hand over three of his grandchildren as hostages for good behaviour. He was not trusted. Perhaps the King was hearing rumours of disaffection from up north; perhaps Northumberland was himself losing patience. Either way, if Northumberland had been innocent of animus against Henry, he no longer was. In fact, he seethed with resentment.

He was so furious that he swallowed his pride enough to make overtures once again to Glendower. Owen Glendower's reputation suffered among the English for his failure to support the Hotspur rebellion. There was a legend that he had climbed a tree at Shelton, having failed to get across the swollen River Severn, to watch the battle to see which way it went. As we have seen, he was actually miles away preparing to attack a royal garrison in west Wales.

But, two years after Shrewsbury, in the summer of 1405, the Percy family tried again, this time with the active support of Glendower. Northumberland also managed to persuade Sir Edmund Mortimer, the father of the claimant to the throne, to act in support of his son. Not only that, but they persuaded the Archbishop of York himself, Richard Scrope, to take part in the rebellion.

In the aftermath, Scrope was captured and beheaded, sending shockwaves throughout Europe that such a senior cleric could be put to death by the civil power. Northumberland himself escaped to Scotland and again, three years later in 1408, he tried one final throw of the dice, leading a Scottish army to invade England. This time he was killed.

The Percy family recovered – they still exist to this day, living in Alnwick Castle on the Northumberland coast – but they have died out twice since. In fact, Hotspur's son, his grandson and his great-grandson all took part on both sides of the Wars of the Roses – and his son Henry lost his life at the Battle of St Albans, the first engagement of that civil war.

Hotspur's wife Katherine, so flirtatious and vivid in Shakespeare's portrayal, married one of Henry IV's most loyal supporters, Thomas Lord Camoys, who commanded the rearguard at Agincourt in 1415. You can still see a splendid brass of them both in their tomb at Trotton in Sussex.

Of the two Scottish aristocrats who played such a role in the battle, George Dunbar Earl of March, was shunned by his fellow Scots because he had sided with Henry, and spent most of the rest of his life intriguing to have his Scottish estates returned – though he died of fever back there, at the grand old age of 82. On the other side, Archibald Earl of Douglas, became a prisoner of the King and was eventually allowed to go home to Scotland on his chivalric honour to return the following Easter. He never did.

Douglas was a real pioneer of the Auld Alliance between Scotland and France, being made Duke of Touraine by the French king Charles VII. He was killed fighting the English at the Battle of Verneuil in Normandy, where the Scots army he led was all but destroyed.

For Henry IV, the Battle of Shrewsbury and its aftermath marked the end of his life as an effective military leader. Some kind of illness took hold of him around 1405 which he found it impossible to shake off. There were unfounded rumours about leprosy, but we know this was not the case because of more recent analysis of his bones. But he was certainly suffering from something and it affected his mind, plunging him into black moods of self-disgust and rage and suspicion of those around him. He began his will with the words: "I Henry, sinful wretch…"

The heavy burden of guilt for seizing the throne and killing God's anointed king, hung heavily on him. From being an extremely wealthy man in his youth, he had turned into a parsimonious King who was unable to balance the books. It was exhausting and debilitating.

Worse, his foulest suspicions fell on his eldest son. Prince Harry was clearly something of a wastrel in his youth, but he was not just a wastrel. He could read and write in English, French and Latin – this was the age of Geoffrey Chaucer, who had worked for Henry's father John of Gaunt. The Prince also wrote music and played the harp. In fact, he carried his harp everywhere with him on campaign.

It isn't clear why his father should start to suspect his eldest son of plotting to seize the throne, except perhaps – in those pre-Freudian days, when it was considered unusual for a father to fear his son – that so many others had been doing so. Prince Harry was replaced on the royal council by his father's favourite son, Thomas, Duke of Clarence.

There is something ironic about the fate of the King. Having harboured such a lust for the throne, he found – once he had achieved it – that his position remained so unsafe, that there could never be any real resolution, to such an extent that he became the living embodiment of fear and suspicion. A little like the man he had replaced.

Henry had lived with a prophecy which had encouraged his ambition to go on crusade, that he would die in Jerusalem. So when he collapsed in Westminster, and was asked when he came round where he was – he was told he was in a room called the Jerusalem Chamber. Shakespeare imagines his reply:

> "Laud be to God! even there my life must end.
> It hath been prophesied to me many years,
> I should not die but in Jerusalem;
> Which vainly I supposed the Holy Land:
> But bear me to that chamber; there I'll lie;
> In that Jerusalem shall Harry die."

Prince Harry succeeded as Henry V and was

determined to become a glorious king, which – in most ways – is how he is remembered by history. But in seizing the throne for the Lancastrians, Henry IV had set in motion a series of disastrous consequences which, as we know, led to prolonged civil war in the next two generations. The Lancastrians and Yorkist descendants of Edward III struggled for supremacy until eight decades after the field of peas outside Shrewsbury, by which time almost nobody who was alive could remember the battle, or could ever remember meeting anyone who had been there.

It is worth wondering for a moment what would have happened if Hotspur had not succumbed to the temptation to rush into the battlefield that evening on St Mary Magdalene's day 1403. What would have happened if he had won the battle and deposed Henry? It would have meant, almost certainly, that young Edmund Mortimer would have been king, perhaps with Hotspur as his regent. It would have meant a very different kind of relationship with Scotland and Wales. It would have meant no Lancastrian dynasty, perhaps no Wars of the Roses, no Agincourt, and no Tudors.

It isn't clear at all what would have happened

instead in the twilight of the medieval centuries or how England would have burst into the new era of Protestantism – though these things were probably inevitable sooner or later. Not even Hotspur could have prevented the rise of Martin Luther. Yet on such minor a turns of the dice, such marginal decisions, history and events are shaped.

As for the Betton family of Upper Berwick, who had looked after Hotspur on his final night, they asked him to leave behind a memento of his visit and he carved the outline of his hand on one of the wooden panels with a knife. It became the family's prized possession, but the subject of yet another prophecy by a local wise woman:

"Whoever by chance shall lose this hand
Will lose both name and house and land."

Sure enough, the Betton family lost the wooden panel during repairs in the nineteenth century and they lost the estate shortly afterwards.

The story of the Battle of Shrewsbury is about the loss of name, house and land. And if the Percy family avoided obliteration for flying in the face of history, they were never quite the powers that they were. But there are so many tales of prophecies fulfilled that we have to make an educated guess that they were part of the fatalistic spirit of the age, and perhaps not surprisingly – those taking part in Shrewsbury had been brought up under the shadow of the Black Death, which had claimed the lives of a third of the population of Europe. It was a generation that believed in fate.

The story of Henry's death in the Jerusalem chamber is a distinctive version of the old classical myths where prophecies were misunderstood and meant the opposite of what they seemed to mean. It is so like the story of Hotspur's prophecy that he would die in Berwick, when he was actually fated to die near Upper Berwick, that you have to wonder how both the main opponents in this battle could both have these delusory prophecies about them.

All we can say is that this too, with its classical allusions – the symptoms as much as anything else of a medieval renaissance – was also, very much, the spirit of the age.

Appendix: Act V of William Shakespeare's *Henry IV Part I*

Enter KING HENRY, PRINCE HENRY, Lord John of LANCASTER, EARL OF WESTMORELAND, SIR WALTER BLUNT, and FALSTAFF]
Henry IV. How bloodily the sun begins to peer
Above yon busky hill! the day looks pale
At his distemperature.
Prince Henry. The southern wind
Doth play the trumpet to his purposes,
And by his hollow whistling in the leaves
Foretells a tempest and a blustering day.
Henry IV. Then with the losers let it sympathize,
For nothing can seem foul to those that win.
[The trumpet sounds]
[Enter WORCESTER and VERNON]

How now, my Lord of Worcester! 'tis not well
That you and I should meet upon such terms
As now we meet. You have deceived our trust,
And made us doff our easy robes of peace,
To crush our old limbs in ungentle steel:
This is not well, my lord, this is not well.
What say you to it? will you again unknit
This curlish knot of all-abhorred war?
And move in that obedient orb again
Where you did give a fair and natural light,
And be no more an exhaled meteor,
A prodigy of fear and a portent
Of broached mischief to the unborn times?
Earl of Worcester. Hear me, my liege:
For mine own part, I could be well content
To entertain the lag-end of my life
With quiet hours; for I do protest,
I have not sought the day of this dislike.
Henry IV. You have not sought it! how comes it, then?
Falstaff. Rebellion lay in his way, and he found it.

Prince Henry. Peace, chewet, peace!
Earl of Worcester. It pleased your majesty to turn your looks
Of favour from myself and all our house;
And yet I must remember you, my lord,
We were the first and dearest of your friends.
For you my staff of office did I break
In Richard's time; and posted day and night
to meet you on the way, and kiss your hand,
When yet you were in place and in account
Nothing so strong and fortunate as I.
It was myself, my brother and his son,
That brought you home and boldly did outdare
The dangers of the time. You swore to us,
And you did swear that oath at Doncaster,
That you did nothing purpose 'gainst the state;
Nor claim no further than your new-fall'n right,
The seat of Gaunt, dukedom of Lancaster:
To this we swore our aid. But in short space
It rain'd down fortune showering on your head;
And such a flood of greatness fell on you,

What with our help, what with the absent king,
What with the injuries of a wanton time,
The seeming sufferances that you had borne,
And the contrarious winds that held the king
So long in his unlucky Irish wars
That all in England did repute him dead:
And from this swarm of fair advantages
You took occasion to be quickly woo'd
To gripe the general sway into your hand;
Forget your oath to us at Doncaster;
And being fed by us you used us so
As that ungentle hull, the cuckoo's bird,
Useth the sparrow; did oppress our nest;
Grew by our feeding to so great a bulk
That even our love durst not come near your sight
For fear of swallowing; but with nimble wing
We were enforced, for safety sake, to fly
Out of sight and raise this present head;
Whereby we stand opposed by such means
As you yourself have forged against yourself
By unkind usage, dangerous countenance,

And violation of all faith and troth
Sworn to us in your younger enterprise.
Henry IV. These things indeed you have articulate,
Proclaim'd at market-crosses, read in churches,
To face the garment of rebellion
With some fine colour that may please the eye
Of fickle changelings and poor discontents,
Which gape and rub the elbow at the news
Of hurlyburly innovation:
And never yet did insurrection want
Such water-colours to impaint his cause;
Nor moody beggars, starving for a time
Of pellmell havoc and confusion.
Prince Henry. In both your armies there is many a soul
Shall pay full dearly for this encounter,
If once they join in trial. Tell your nephew,
The Prince of Wales doth join with all the world
In praise of Henry Percy: by my hopes,
This present enterprise set off his head,

I do not think a braver gentleman,
More active-valiant or more valiant-young,
More daring or more bold, is now alive
To grace this latter age with noble deeds.
For my part, I may speak it to my shame,
I have a truant been to chivalry;
And so I hear he doth account me too;
Yet this before my father's majesty—
I am content that he shall take the odds
Of his great name and estimation,
And will, to save the blood on either side,
Try fortune with him in a single fight.
Henry IV. And, Prince of Wales, so dare we venture thee,
Albeit considerations infinite
Do make against it. No, good Worcester, no,
We love our people well; even those we love
That are misled upon your cousin's part;
And, will they take the offer of our grace,
Both he and they and you, every man
Shall be my friend again and I'll be his:

So tell your cousin, and bring me word
What he will do: but if he will not yield,
Rebuke and dread correction wait on us
And they shall do their office. So, be gone;
We will not now be troubled with reply:
We offer fair; take it advisedly.
[Exeunt WORCESTER and VERNON]
Prince Henry. It will not be accepted, on my life:
The Douglas and the Hotspur both together
Are confident against the world in arms.
Henry IV. Hence, therefore, every leader to his charge;
For, on their answer, will we set on them:
And God befriend us, as our cause is just!
[Exeunt all but PRINCE HENRY and FALSTAFF]
Falstaff. Hal, if thou see me down in the battle and bestride
me, so; 'tis a point of friendship.
Prince Henry. Nothing but a colossus can do thee that friendship.

Say thy prayers, and farewell.
Falstaff. I would 'twere bed-time, Hal, and all well.
Prince Henry. Why, thou owest God a death.
[Exit PRINCE HENRY]
Falstaff. 'Tis not due yet; I would be loath to pay him before
his day. What need I be so forward with him that
calls not on me? Well, 'tis no matter; honour pricks
me on. Yea, but how if honour prick me off when I
come on? how then? Can honour set to a leg? no: or
an arm? no: or take away the grief of a wound? no.
Honour hath no skill in surgery, then? no. What is
honour? a word. What is in that word honour? what
is that honour? air. A trim reckoning! Who hath it?
he that died o' Wednesday. Doth he feel it? no.
Doth he hear it? no. 'Tis insensible, then. Yea,

to the dead. But will it not live with the living?
no. Why? detraction will not suffer it. Therefore
I'll none of it. Honour is a mere scutcheon: and so
ends my catechism.
[Exit]

Act V, Scene 2
The rebel camp.

[Enter WORCESTER and VERNON]

Earl of Worcester. O, no, my nephew must not know, Sir Richard,
The liberal and kind offer of the king.
Vernon. 'Twere best he did.
Earl of Worcester. Then are we all undone.
It is not possible, it cannot be,
The king should keep his word in loving us;
He will suspect us still and find a time
To punish this offence in other faults:
Suspicion all our lives shall be stuck full of eyes;
For treason is but trusted like the fox,
Who, ne'er so tame, so cherish'd and lock'd up,
Will have a wild trick of his ancestors.
Look how we can, or sad or merrily,
Interpretation will misquote our looks,
And we shall feed like oxen at a stall,
The better cherish'd, still the nearer death.

My nephew's trespass may be well forgot;
it hath the excuse of youth and heat of blood,
And an adopted name of privilege,
A hair-brain'd Hotspur, govern'd by a spleen:
All his offences live upon my head
And on his father's; we did train him on,
And, his corruption being ta'en from us,
We, as the spring of all, shall pay for all.
Therefore, good cousin, let not Harry know,
In any case, the offer of the king.
Vernon. Deliver what you will; I'll say 'tis so.
Here comes your cousin.
[Enter HOTSPUR and DOUGLAS]
Hotspur. My uncle is return'd:
Deliver up my Lord of Westmoreland.
Uncle, what news?
Earl of Worcester. The king will bid you battle presently.
Earl of Douglas. Defy him by the Lord of Westmoreland.
Hotspur. Lord Douglas, go you and tell him so.

Earl of Douglas. Marry, and shall, and very willingly.
[Exit]
Earl of Worcester. There is no seeming mercy in the king.
Hotspur. Did you beg any? God forbid!
Earl of Worcester. I told him gently of our grievances,
Of his oath-breaking; which he mended thus,
By now forswearing that he is forsworn:
He calls us rebels, traitors; and will scourge
With haughty arms this hateful name in us.
[Re-enter the EARL OF DOUGLAS]
Earl of Douglas. Arm, gentlemen; to arms! for I have thrown
A brave defiance in King Henry's teeth,
And Westmoreland, that was engaged, did bear it;
Which cannot choose but bring him quickly on.
Earl of Worcester. The Prince of Wales stepp'd forth before the king,
And, nephew, challenged you to single fight.

Hotspur. O, would the quarrel lay upon our heads,
And that no man might draw short breath today
But I and Harry Monmouth! Tell me, tell me,
How show'd his tasking? seem'd it in contempt?
Vernon. No, by my soul; I never in my life
Did hear a challenge urged more modestly,
Unless a brother should a brother dare
To gentle exercise and proof of arms.
He gave you all the duties of a man;
Trimm'd up your praises with a princely tongue,
Spoke to your deservings like a chronicle,
Making you ever better than his praise
By still dispraising praise valued in you;
And, which became him like a prince indeed,
He made a blushing cital of himself;
And chid his truant youth with such a grace
As if he master'd there a double spirit.
Of teaching and of learning instantly.
There did he pause: but let me tell the world,
If he outlive the envy of this day,

England did never owe so sweet a hope,
So much misconstrued in his wantonness.
Hotspur. Cousin, I think thou art enamoured
On his follies: never did I hear
Of any prince so wild a libertine.
But be he as he will, yet once ere night
I will embrace him with a soldier's arm,
That he shall shrink under my courtesy.
Arm, arm with speed: and, fellows, soldiers, friends,
Better consider what you have to do
Than I, that have not well the gift of tongue,
Can lift your blood up with persuasion.
[Enter a Messenger]
Messenger. My lord, here are letters for you.
Hotspur. I cannot read them now.
O gentlemen, the time of life is short!
To spend that shortness basely were too long,
If life did ride upon a dial's point,
Still ending at the arrival of an hour.
An if we live, we live to tread on kings;

If die, brave death, when princes die with us!
Now, for our consciences, the arms are fair,
When the intent of bearing them is just.
[Enter another Messenger]
Messenger. My lord, prepare; the king comes on apace.
Hotspur. I thank him, that he cuts me from my tale,
For I profess not talking; only this—
Let each man do his best: and here draw I
A sword, whose temper I intend to stain
With the best blood that I can meet withal
In the adventure of this perilous day.
Now, Esperance! Percy! and set on.
Sound all the lofty instruments of war,
And by that music let us all embrace;
For, heaven to earth, some of us never shall
A second time do such a courtesy.
[The trumpets sound. They embrace, and exeunt]

Act V, Scene 3
Plain between the camps.

[KING HENRY enters with his power. Alarum to the battle. Then enter DOUGLAS and SIR WALTER BLUNT]

Blunt. What is thy name, that in the battle thus
Thou crossest me? what honour dost thou seek
Upon my head?
Earl of Douglas. Know then, my name is Douglas;
And I do haunt thee in the battle thus
Because some tell me that thou art a king.
Blunt. They tell thee true.
Earl of Douglas. The Lord of Stafford dear to-day hath bought
Thy likeness, for instead of thee, King Harry,
This sword hath ended him: so shall it thee,
Unless thou yield thee as my prisoner.
Blunt. I was not born a yielder, thou proud Scot;
And thou shalt find a king that will revenge

Lord Stafford's death.
[They fight. DOUGLAS kills SIR WALTER BLUNT.
Enter HOTSPUR]
Hotspur. O Douglas, hadst thou fought at Holmedon thus,
never had triumph'd upon a Scot.
Earl of Douglas. All's done, all's won; here breathless lies the king.
Hotspur. Where?
Earl of Douglas. Here.
Hotspur. This, Douglas? no: I know this face full well:
A gallant knight he was, his name was Blunt;
Semblably furnish'd like the king himself.
Earl of Douglas. A fool go with thy soul, whither it goes!
A borrow'd title hast thou bought too dear:
Why didst thou tell me that thou wert a king?
Hotspur. The king hath many marching in his coats.

Earl of Douglas. Now, by my sword, I will kill all his coats;
I'll murder all his wardrobe, piece by piece,
Until I meet the king.
Hotspur. Up, and away!
Our soldiers stand full fairly for the day.
[Exeunt]
[Alarum. Enter FALSTAFF, solus]
Falstaff. Though I could 'scape shot-free at London, I fear
the shot here; here's no scoring but upon the pate. Soft! who are you? Sir Walter Blunt: there's honour
for you! here's no vanity! I am as hot as moulten lead, and as heavy too: God keep lead out of me! I need no more weight than mine own bowels. I have
led my ragamuffins where they are peppered: there's
not three of my hundred and fifty left alive; and they are for the town's end, to beg during life.

But who comes here?

[Enter PRINCE HENRY]

Prince Henry. What, stand'st thou idle here? lend me thy sword:
Many a nobleman lies stark and stiff
Under the hoofs of vaunting enemies,
Whose deaths are yet unrevenged: I prithee, lend me thy sword.

Falstaff. O Hal, I prithee, give me leave to breathe awhile.
Turk Gregory never did such deeds in arms as I have
done this day. I have paid Percy, I have made him sure.

Prince Henry. He is, indeed; and living to kill thee. I prithee,
lend me thy sword.

Falstaff. Nay, before God, Hal, if Percy be alive, thou get'st
not my sword; but take my pistol, if thou wilt.

Prince Henry. Give it to me: what, is it in the

case?

Falstaff. Ay, Hal; 'tis hot, 'tis hot; there's that will sack a city.

[PRINCE HENRY draws it out, and finds it to be a bottle of sack]

Prince Henry. What, is it a time to jest and dally now?**2940**

[He throws the bottle at him. Exit]

Falstaff. Well, if Percy be alive, I'll pierce him. If he do
come in my way, so: if he do not, if I come in his willingly, let him make a carbonado of me. I like not such grinning honour as Sir Walter hath: give me **2945**
life: which if I can save, so; if not, honour comes unlooked for, and there's an end.

[Exit FALSTAFF]

Act V, Scene 4
Another part of the field.

[Alarum. Excursions. Enter PRINCE HENRY, LORD JOHN OF LANCASTER, and EARL OF WESTMORELAND]

Henry IV. I prithee,
Harry, withdraw thyself; thou bleed'st too much.
Lord John of Lancaster, go you with him.

Prince John. Not I, my lord, unless I did bleed too.

Prince Henry. I beseech your majesty, make up,
Lest your retirement do amaze your friends.

Henry IV. I will do so.
My Lord of Westmoreland, lead him to his tent.

Earl of Westmoreland. Come, my lord, I'll lead you to your tent.

Prince Henry. Lead me, my lord? I do not need your help:
And God forbid a shallow scratch should drive
The Prince of Wales from such a field as this,

Where stain'd nobility lies trodden on,
and rebels' arms triumph in massacres!
Prince John. We breathe too long: come, cousin Westmoreland,
Our duty this way lies; for God's sake come.
[Exeunt LANCASTER and WESTMORELAND]
Prince Henry. By God, thou hast deceived me, Lancaster;
I did not think thee lord of such a spirit:
Before, I loved thee as a brother, John;
But now, I do respect thee as my soul.
Henry IV. I saw him hold Lord Percy at the point
With lustier maintenance than I did look for
Of such an ungrown warrior.
Prince Henry. O, this boy
Lends mettle to us all!
[Exit]
[Enter DOUGLAS]
Earl of Douglas. Another king! they grow like Hydra's heads:
I am the Douglas, fatal to all those

That wear those colours on them: what art thou,
That counterfeit'st the person of a king?
Henry IV. The king himself; who, Douglas, grieves at heart
So many of his shadows thou hast met
And not the very king. I have two boys
Seek Percy and thyself about the field:
But, seeing thou fall'st on me so luckily,
I will assay thee: so, defend thyself.
Earl of Douglas. I fear thou art another counterfeit;
And yet, in faith, thou bear'st thee like a king:
But mine I am sure thou art, whoe'er thou be,
And thus I win thee.
[They fight. KING HENRY being in danger, PRINCE HENRY enters]
Prince Henry. Hold up thy head, vile Scot, or thou art like
Never to hold it up again! the spirits
Of valiant Shirley, Stafford, Blunt, are in my arms:
It is the Prince of Wales that threatens thee;

Who never promiseth but he means to pay.
[They fight: DOUGLAS flies]
Cheerly, my lord. how fares your grace?
Sir Nicholas Gawsey hath for succor sent,
And so hath Clifton: I'll to Clifton straight.
Henry IV. Stay, and breathe awhile:
Thou hast redeem'd thy lost opinion,
And show'd thou makest some tender of my life,
In this fair rescue thou hast brought to me.
Prince Henry. O God! they did me too much injury
That ever said I hearken'd for your death.
If it were so, I might have let alone
The insulting hand of Douglas over you,
Which would have been as speedy in your end
As all the poisonous potions in the world
And saved the treacherous labour of your son.
Henry IV. Make up to Clifton: I'll to Sir Nicholas Gawsey.
[Exit]
[Enter HOTSPUR]

Hotspur. If I mistake not, thou art Harry Monmouth.
Prince Henry. Thou speak'st as if I would deny my name.
Hotspur. My name is Harry Percy.
Prince Henry. Why, then I see
A very valiant rebel of the name.
I am the Prince of Wales; and think not, Percy,
To share with me in glory any more:
Two stars keep not their motion in one sphere;
Nor can one England brook a double reign,
Of Harry Percy and the Prince of Wales.
Hotspur. Nor shall it, Harry; for the hour is come
To end the one of us; and would to God
Thy name in arms were now as great as mine!
Prince Henry. I'll make it greater ere I part from thee;
And all the budding honours on thy crest
I'll crop, to make a garland for my head.
Hotspur. I can no longer brook thy vanities.
[They fight]

[Enter FALSTAFF]

Falstaff. Well said, Hal! to it Hal! Nay, you shall find no
boy's play here, I can tell you.
[Re-enter DOUGLAS; he fights with FALSTAFF,]
who falls down as if he were dead, and exit
DOUGLAS. HOTSPUR is wounded, and falls]
Hotspur. O, Harry, thou hast robb'd me of my youth!
I better brook the loss of brittle life
Than those proud titles thou hast won of me;
They wound my thoughts worse than sword my flesh:
But thought's the slave of life, and life time's fool;
And time, that takes survey of all the world,
Must have a stop. O, I could prophesy,
But that the earthy and cold hand of death
Lies on my tongue: no, Percy, thou art dust
And food for—
[Dies]
Prince Henry. For worms, brave Percy: fare thee

well, great heart!
Ill-weaved ambition, how much art thou shrunk!
When that this body did contain a spirit,
A kingdom for it was too small a bound;
But now two paces of the vilest earth
Is room enough: this earth that bears thee dead
Bears not alive so stout a gentleman.
If thou wert sensible of courtesy,
I should not make so dear a show of zeal:
But let my favours hide thy mangled face;
And, even in thy behalf, I'll thank myself
For doing these fair rites of tenderness.
Adieu, and take thy praise with thee to heaven!
Thy ignominy sleep with thee in the grave,
But not remember'd in thy epitaph!
[He spieth FALSTAFF on the ground]
What, old acquaintance! could not all this flesh
Keep in a little life? Poor Jack, farewell!
I could have better spared a better man:
O, I should have a heavy miss of thee,
If I were much in love with vanity!

Death hath not struck so fat a deer to-day,
Though many dearer, in this bloody fray.
Embowell'd will I see thee by and by:
Till then in blood by noble Percy lie.
[Exit PRINCE HENRY]
Falstaff. *[Rising up]* Embowelled! if thou embowel me to-day,
I'll give you leave to powder me and eat me too to-morrow. 'Sblood,'twas time to counterfeit, or that hot termagant Scot had paid me scot and lot too.
Counterfeit? I lie, I am no counterfeit: to die, is to be a counterfeit; for he is but the counterfeit of a man who hath not the life of a man: but to counterfeit dying, when a man thereby liveth, is to be no counterfeit, but the true and perfect image of life indeed. The better part of valour is discretion; in the which better part I have saved my life. 'Zounds, I am afraid of this gunpowder Percy, though he be dead: how, if he should counterfeit too and rise? by my faith, I am

afraid he would prove the better counterfeit.
Therefore I'll make him sure; yea, and I'll swear I
killed him. Why may not he rise as well as I?
Nothing confutes me but eyes, and nobody sees me.
Therefore, sirrah,
[Stabbing him]
with a new wound in your thigh, come you along
with me.
[Takes up HOTSPUR on his back]
[Re-enter PRINCE HENRY and LORD JOHN OF LANCASTER]
Prince Henry. Come, brother John; full bravely hast thou flesh'd
Thy maiden sword.
Prince John. But, soft! whom have we here?
Did you not tell me this fat man was dead?
Prince Henry. I did; I saw him dead,
Breathless and bleeding on the ground. Art thou alive?
Or is it fantasy that plays upon our eyesight?
I prithee, speak; we will not trust our eyes

Without our ears: thou art not what thou seem'st.
Falstaff. No, that's certain; I am not a double man: but if I
be not Jack Falstaff, then am I a Jack. There is Percy:
[Throwing the body down]
if your father will do me any honour, so; if not, let
him kill the next Percy himself. I look to be either
earl or duke, I can assure you.
Prince Henry. Why, Percy I killed myself and saw thee dead.
Falstaff. Didst thou? Lord, Lord, how this world is given to
lying! I grant you I was down and out of breath;
and so was he: but we rose both at an instant and
fought a long hour by Shrewsbury clock. If I may be
believed, so; if not, let them that should reward
valour bear the sin upon their own heads. I'll take
it upon my death, I gave him this wound in the
thigh: if the man were alive and would deny it,
'zounds, I would make him eat a piece of my sword.

Prince John. This is the strangest tale that ever I heard.

Prince Henry. This is the strangest fellow, brother John.
Come, bring your luggage nobly on your back:
For my part, if a lie may do thee grace,
I'll gild it with the happiest terms I have.
[A retreat is sounded]
The trumpet sounds retreat; the day is ours.
Come, brother, let us to the highest of the field,
To see what friends are living, who are dead.
[Exeunt PRINCE HENRY and LANCASTER]

Falstaff. I'll follow, as they say, for reward. He that rewards me, God reward him! If I do grow great, I'll grow less; for I'll purge, and leave sack, and live cleanly as a nobleman should do.
[Exit]

Act V, Scene 5
Another part of the field.

[The trumpets sound. Enter KING HENRY IV, PRINCE HENRY, LORD JOHN LANCASTER, EARL OF WESTMORELAND, with WORCESTER and VERNON prisoners]

Henry IV. Thus ever did rebellion find rebuke.
Ill-spirited Worcester! did not we send grace,
Pardon and terms of love to all of you?
And wouldst thou turn our offers contrary?
Misuse the tenor of thy kinsman's trust?
Three knights upon our party slain to-day,
A noble earl and many a creature else
Had been alive this hour,
If like a Christian thou hadst truly borne
Betwixt our armies true intelligence.

Earl of Worcester. What I have done my safety urged me to;
And I embrace this fortune patiently,

Since not to be avoided it falls on me.
Henry IV. Bear Worcester to the death and Vernon too:
Other offenders we will pause upon.
[Exeunt WORCESTER and VERNON, guarded]
How goes the field?
Prince Henry. The noble Scot, Lord Douglas, when he saw
The fortune of the day quite turn'd from him,
The noble Percy slain, and all his men
Upon the foot of fear, fled with the rest;
And falling from a hill, he was so bruised
That the pursuers took him. At my tent
The Douglas is; and I beseech your grace
I may dispose of him.
Henry IV. With all my heart.
Prince Henry. Then, brother John of Lancaster, to you
This honourable bounty shall belong:
Go to the Douglas, and deliver him
Up to his pleasure, ransomless and free:

His valour shown upon our crests to-day
Hath taught us how to cherish such high deeds
Even in the bosom of our adversaries.
Prince John. I thank your grace for this high courtesy,
Which I shall give away immediately.
Henry IV. Then this remains, that we divide our power.
You, son John, and my cousin Westmoreland
Towards York shall bend you with your dearest speed,
To meet Northumberland and the prelate Scroop,
Who, as we hear, are busily in arms:
Myself and you, son Harry, will towards Wales,
To fight with Glendower and the Earl of March.
Rebellion in this land shall lose his sway,
Meeting the cheque of such another day:
And since this business so fair is done,
Let us not leave till all our own be won.
[Exeunt]

Friends of Battlefield Church

This large, dignified church stands in open countryside on the site of the ferocious Battle of Shrewsbury, which took place in 1403.

Thousands of soldiers are thought to have died in the fray, and the church remains a quiet, some would say melancholic, memorial to the 1,600 people who were said to have been buried there. A statue of Henry IV, who defeated Henry "Hotspur" Percy in the battle, stands on the outside east wall. On the roof beams inside are representations of the shields of the knights who fought with Henry IV. A service is still held each year in July to commemorate the anniversary of the battle.

Much of the church we see today is the result of an extensive restoration in the 1860s, by a distinguished local architect S Pountney Smith, who saved the church from ruin. Though he kept the original shape, tower and walls, the magnificent hammerbeam roof, the reredos, and all the fittings and furniture were installed by him.

He was also responsible for installing the fine stained glass typical of the 1860s.

Especially memorable is the east window with its wonderful palette of colours. One particular treasure is the Pieta, carved in oak, showing the Virgin Mary holding Christ's body. It is a remarkable and moving piece dating from the fifteenth century and thought to have been brought here from another church.

https://www.visitchurches.org.uk/visit/church-listing/st-mary-magdalene-battlefield.html

Further reading

Juliet Barker (2005), *Agincourt: The king, the campaign, the battle,* London: Little Brown.

Richard Britnell and John Hatcher (eds.) (1996) *Progress and Problems in Medieval England: Essays in Honour of Edward Miller,* Cambridge, CUP.

Gordon Corrigan (2013), *A Great and Glorious Adventure: A military history of the Hundred Years War,* London: Atlantic Books.

Anne Curry, (2015), *Agincourt,* Oxford, OUP.

Alistair Dunn (2003), 'A kingdom in crisis: Henry IV and the Battle of Shrewsbury', *History Today,* Vol 53, Issue 8, August.

W. G. D. Fletcher (1903) Battlefield Church, Salop and the Battle of Shrewsbury, 2nd edition, Shrewsbury: Adentt and Naunton.

Chris Given-Wilson (2016), *Henry IV*, New Haven: Yale University Press.

David Green (2014), *The Hundred Years War: A People's History*, New Haven: Yale University Press.

Philip Morgan (2003), *The Battle of Shrewsbury 1403*, Stroud: History Press.

Michael Prestwich (1996), *Armies and Warfare in the Middle Ages: the English Experience*, New Haven: Yale University Press,

E. J. Priestley (1979), *The Battle of Shrewsbury 1403*, Shrewsbury and Atcham Borough Council.

Stephen Maxfield (2003), *The Battlefield of Shrewsbury*, Self-published.

B. Wilkinson (1969), *The Later Middle Ages in England 1216-1485*, London: Longman.